FROM
CANDLE
TO
QUARTZ CLOCK

The story of time and timekeeping

by Anita Ganeri

Published by Evans Brothers Limited
2A Portman Mansions
Chiltern Street
London W1M 1LE

© copyright Evans Brothers Limited 1996

British Library Cataloguing in Publication data.
A catalogue record for this book is available from the British Library.

First published 1996

Reprinted 1998

Printed in Hong Kong by Wing King Tong Co. Ltd

0 237 51534 2

Acknowledgements

Editor: Nicola Barber

Design: Neil Sayer

Illustrations: Hardlines

Production: Jenny Mulvanny

Acknowledgements

The author and publishers would like to thank the following for permission to reproduce photographs:
Front cover: (top right) Victor Watts, Robert Harding Picture Library (top left) Bonhams, London, Bridgeman Art Library (centre) Science Museum, Science and Society Picture Library (bottom left) Victor Watts, Robert Harding Picture Library (bottom right) Robert Harding Picture Library
Back cover: Seth Joel, Science Photo Library
Title page: Science Museum, Science and Society Picture Library
page 6 (left) David Parker, Science Photo Library, (right) Bonhams, London, The Bridgeman Art Library, (bottom) SNCF page 7 (top) Hulton Deutsch Collection Limited, (bottom) Photo Library Int., Robert Harding Picture Library page 8 John Sanford, Science Photo Library page 9 (top) British Museum, The Bridgeman Art Library, (bottom) Adam Hart-Davis, Science Photo Library page 10 (top) NASA, Science Photo Library, (bottom) Michael Marten, Science Photo Library page 11 (top) Simon Fraser, Science Photo Library, (bottom) Giraudon, The Bridgeman Art Library page 12 (top) British Museum, (bottom) Pegasus Partners Ltd. page 13 (left) British Museum, The Bridgeman Art Library, (right) Tim Dackus, Robert Harding Picture Library page 14 (top) Hulton Deutsch Collection Limited, (bottom) Robert Harding Picture Library page 15 The Bridgeman Art Library page 16 David Parker, Science Photo Library page 17 (middle) National Museum of Anthropology, Mexico, Werner Forman Archive, (bottom) Private collection, The Bridgeman Art Library page 18 (top) Ronald Sheridan, Ancient Art & Architecture Collection, (bottom) Hulton Deutsch Collection Limited page 19 (left) Private collection, The Bridgeman Art Library, (right) Mary Evans Picture Library page 20 (left) Ronald Sheridan, Ancient Art & Architecture Collection, (right) Robert Harding Picture Library page 21 (left) H. Rogers, Trip, (right) Robert Frerck, Robert Harding Picture Library page 22 (top) Science Museum, Science & Society Picture Library, (bottom) Werner Forman Archive page 23 (top and bottom) Science Museum, Science & Society Picture Library, (middle) ZEFA page 24 (top) Salisbury Cathedral, The Bridgeman Art Library, (bottom) Science Museum, London, The Bridgeman Art Library page 25 (top) Image Select, Ann Ronan, (bottom) Christie's, London, The Bridgeman Art Library page 26 (top) Crellin, London, Mary Evans Picture Library, (bottom) Science Museum, Science & Society Picture Library page 27 (top) Glyn Kirk, Action-Plus Photographic, (middle) Image Select, Ann Ronan, (bottom) Alexander Tsiaras, Science Photo Library.

CONTENTS

TIME ON OUR HANDS

Second by second, minute by minute, month by month and year by year, time is constantly passing. How often do you look at a watch or clock during the day? Count up, and you might be surprised!

From the moment we wake up, most of us are aware of the time. Time rules our lives, telling us when to get up, when to go to school or work, when to catch the bus, eat our meals, meet our friends and go to bed.

An electronic stopwatch

WHAT'S THE TIME?

In our modern homes, cars and offices we are surrounded by timepieces – watches, timers on videos and cookers, diaries, calendars and clocks of all shapes and sizes. It is hard to imagine a world without them. But it wasn't always like this. Our ancient ancestors had no such devices for telling the time. These were invented as society developed and began to be better organised.

A beautiful 17th-century 'grandfather' clock

SIGNPOST

The practical applications of measuring the time are all around us. Timetables, such as bus, train and school timetables, help to keep our lives running smoothly and allow us to plan our time. Without this type of organisation, modern life would become extremely confusing and chaotic!

A French train timetable

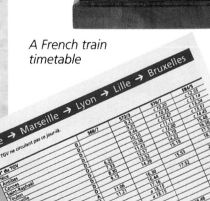

OLD FATHER TIME

The Ancient Egyptians and Ancient Greeks worshipped time as a god. But other views of time were rather more gloomy. In the Middle Ages, people pictured time as a figure who carried an hourglass and a scythe. This figure was known as Old Father Time, and his appearance signalled someone's death. The hourglass meant that the sands of time had run out for the victim, and the scythe was for cutting the victim's life short.

Old Father Time

PAST, PRESENT AND FUTURE

Most languages have plenty of words for describing what has happened in the past, what is happening at present and what might happen in the future. But different peoples have different ways of understanding and expressing time. The Hopi Indians of the USA don't use special words for past, present or future events. Instead, they talk about time as what happens 'when the corn ripens' or 'when the great storm blows'.

THE BEGINNING OF TIME

In 1656 an Irish archbishop, James Ussher, announced that the Earth had been created at 10 a.m. on Saturday, 3 October, 4004 BC. He calculated this date from information in the Bible. At around the same time, a Polish astronomer, Johannes Hevelius, calculated the exact date of creation to be 6 p.m. on 24 October, 3963 BC. He worked his date out from the stars.

IN FACT...

In fact, scientists have worked out that the Earth is 4,600 million years old! The first living things appeared on Earth some 3,200 million years ago. But the first human beings did not appear until just two million years ago.

Planet Earth

LIFE BEFORE CLOCKS

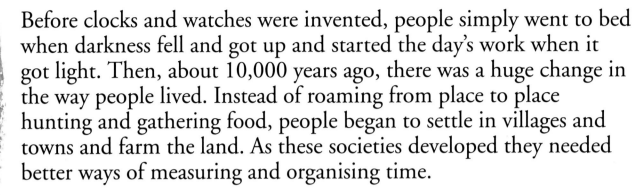

Before clocks and watches were invented, people simply went to bed when darkness fell and got up and started the day's work when it got light. Then, about 10,000 years ago, there was a huge change in the way people lived. Instead of roaming from place to place hunting and gathering food, people began to settle in villages and towns and farm the land. As these societies developed they needed better ways of measuring and organising time.

NATURAL CLOCKS

Early people did not need to measure time in any great detail. They simply observed the passing of the days and nights, and the changing of the seasons. The Sun, Moon and stars were their only clocks. The rising and setting of the Sun marked the beginning and end of a day. The phases of the Moon showed the passing months. Ancient astronomers would climb to the top of a mountain and wait for the Moon to rise in order to see if it was the start of a new month or the end of an old one.

Three phases of the Moon – from waxing (top), to full (middle), to crescent (bottom)

SIGNPOST

The Ancient Egyptians based the beginning of their year on the time when a star called Sirius (the Dog Star) rose just before daybreak. At the same time as Sirius appeared in the morning sky, the River Nile flooded. This was an important annual event for Egyptian farmers. The rich soil deposited by the floodwaters allowed the farmers to grow a wide variety of crops. Without the floods, the land would have been too poor to farm.

EARLY ASTRONOMERS

The heavenly bodies were not only used as clocks. As long ago as 1500 BC, Babylonian astronomer-priests were studying the heavens in order to try to predict the appearance of unlucky omens, such as eclipses of the Sun or Moon, and to tell what the future held in store. Their knowledge of the skies made these astronomer-priests very powerful, because ordinary people believed that their destinies were controlled by the movements of the stars, Moon and planets.

A Babylonian stone tablet used by astronomer-priests for calculating the movements of the planet Jupiter

FOOD FOR THE STARS

The Aborigines of Australia traditionally lived by hunting and gathering food. They told the time by linking the positions of the Sun, Moon and stars with good or bad weather, or with particular types of seasonal food. One tribe knew that when a star called Marpeankurrk appeared in the north in the evening, the time had come to gather wood-ant larvae, a great delicacy.

A dandelion flower early in the morning (above) and at midday (right)

IN FACT...

Many plants have a kind of built-in clock which tells them the time of day and the time of year. This clock controls the plant's flowers, making sure that they open at times when they stand the greatest chance of being pollinated. For example, some daisies and dandelions have flowers that close at night and open during the day. Animals have body clocks, too. This is how birds know when to migrate and small mammals know when to wake up after their winter hibernation.

DAYS, MONTHS AND YEARS

As civilisations grew larger, people needed more accurate units of time in order to record past events, measure the present, and plan for the future. Many of the units we use today to measure time are based on the calculations of these early peoples, using the natural divisions caused by the movements of the Sun, Moon and Earth in relation to each other. This is how we get days, months and years.

The Earth and the Moon seen together in space

DAYS AND NIGHTS

A full day and night is the time it takes for the Earth to spin once on its axis, an imaginary line running through the centre of the Earth from north to south. As it spins, one half of the Earth faces the Sun and has daylight. The other half faces away from the Sun and has night.

WHEN DOES DAY BEGIN?

Different people had different ideas about when day began. The Ancient Egyptian day began at dawn. For the Babylonians, Jews and Muslims, day began at dusk. The Ancient Romans decreed that day began at midnight, and this is still the case today.

IN FACT...

Because the Earth's spin is gradually slowing down, each day is 0.00000002 seconds longer than the one before. On a daily basis, the difference is far too small to notice. But it means that every 7,500 years a whole day will be lost.

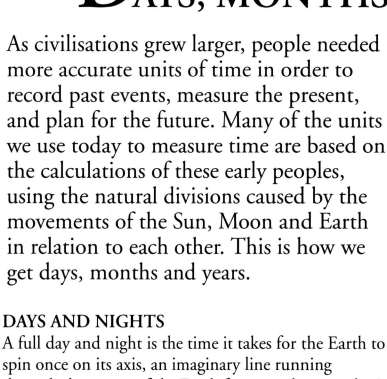

The Ancient Egyptians believed that the day began as the Sun rose at dawn.

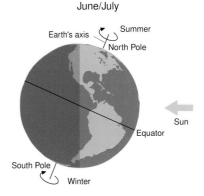

June/July

Earth's axis — Summer
North Pole

Sun

Equator

South Pole — Winter

December/January

Earth's axis — Winter
North Pole

Equator

Sun

South Pole — Summer

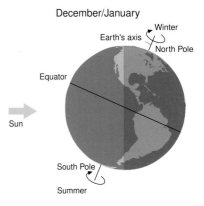

The Earth tilts on its axis as it spins. As a result, one pole is constantly facing towards the Sun in summer, and the other away from the Sun in winter.

THE MIDNIGHT SUN

In June and July, the North Pole has constant daylight, 24 hours a day. Meanwhile, it is permanently dark at the South Pole. In December and January, the South Pole becomes the 'land of the midnight Sun'.

YEARS AND MONTHS

A year is based on the time it takes for the Earth to travel once around the Sun, which is 365 days, 5 hours, 48 minutes and 45.9747 seconds. This is called a solar year. A month is based on the time it takes for the Moon to travel around the Earth, which is approximately 27.3 days.

Julius Caesar

NAMING THE MONTHS

The names of the months have come down to us from Roman times, because it was Julius Caesar who invented the calendar on which ours is based. He gave important months 31 days and less important ones 30 days. Important months were named after Roman gods, such as January (after Janus, god of beginnings) and March (after Mars, god of war). July was named after Caesar himself.

IN FACT...

On Mercury, the planet closest to the Sun, a day lasts for 58.7 Earth days (the time it takes for Mercury to spin once on its axis). A Mercury year is 88 Earth days long (the time it takes for Mercury to orbit the Sun). On Pluto, the planet furthest from the Sun, a day lasts for 6.4 Earth days. But a Pluto year is the equivalent to 248 Earth years.

UNITS OF TIME

After years and months, time is divided up further into weeks, and smaller units such as hours, minutes and seconds. These are not natural divisions. Over thousands of years, people have fixed and standardised these units for greater accuracy and convenience.

The strokes and dashes on this clay tablet represent Sumerian numbers.

DIVIDED BY 60

Hours were first divided into 60 minutes, and minutes into 60 seconds by the Sumerians, a people who lived in Iraq some 5,000 years ago. The Sumerians invented one of the world's first written number systems. They based this system on counting in 60s (instead of tens as in the decimal system), because 60 is easy to divide by two, three and four.

DAYS OF THE WEEK

The Babylonians were the first to use a seven-day week, now standard throughout the world. They named the days after the seven planets known at the time. The Ancient Greeks divided the month into three ten-day parts but the seven-day week was reinstated by the Romans.

BREAKTHROUGH

The first people to divide the day into 24 parts were the Ancient Egyptians. Daylight and darkness were each split into 12 'hours'. But as the length of the day and night changed throughout the year, so did the length of the 'hours'. It was the Babylonians in about 3000 BC who made all 24 hours equal in length. Equal hours did not become standard in Europe until AD 1350.

For many people, the seven-day week is divided into a five-day working week and a two-day weekend.

Avril-April-April

8
Lundi - Maandag
Montag - Monday
Lunedì - Lunes

9
Mardi - Dinsdag
Dienstag - Tuesday
Martedì - Martes

10
Mercredi - Woensdag
Mittwoch - Wednesday
Mercoledì - Miércoles

In English, the days of the week are named after the Sun, the Moon, and various gods and goddesses.

Monday: named after the Moon
Tuesday: named after Tiu, Anglo-Saxon god of war
Wednesday: named after Woden, chief Anglo-Saxon god
Thursday: named after Thor, Norse god of sky and thunder
Friday: named after Fria, Norse goddess of love
Saturday: named after Roman god, Saturn

A silver pocket watch from France. It has a decimal face, for showing time in units of ten.

SIGNPOST

The Nuer people of Sudan in Africa do not use hours, minutes and seconds to measure time. Instead, they think in terms of important events and happenings, often involving their herds of cattle. For example, they might talk of the time when 'the herds go to water' or when 'the cattle give birth to their young'.

A.M. AND P.M.

The Romans described the hours before midday as *antemeridiem*, 'before noon', and the hours after midday as *postmeridiem*, 'after noon'. We still use their abbreviated forms, a.m. and p.m., for morning and afternoon.

TIMING IN TENS

In 1792, a new calendar was introduced to celebrate the end of the French Revolution and the beginning of the French Republic. It had a 10-day week, a 10-hour day, a 100-minute hour and a 100-second minute. It was not very successful. By 1795, it had been scrapped altogether.

TIME ZONES

Until just over 100 years ago, the time shown by clocks could vary wildly from place to place. It was not simply different countries that used different times. The time in one town might be completely different from the time a few kilometres away. But this all changed with the growth of industry and better transport systems in the 19th century.

WORLD TIME ZONES

Today, the world is divided into 24 time zones, each with a different time of day. As you go west, you lose an hour for each time zone you cross. As you go east, you gain an hour. Some large countries cover several time zones.

AGREEING ON TIME

The system of time zones used today was decided at the International Meridian Conference in Washington, USA, in 1884. This system was agreed in order to avoid small, local time differences and to make sure that all countries have noon in the middle of the day. The starting point for the time zones is Greenwich, London. All the clocks within each zone tell the same time and each zone is a whole number of hours ahead of or behind the zones to the east or west of it. The only exceptions are countries such as India, which is 5.5 hours ahead of Greenwich time.

SIGNPOST

Until 1880, many different local time zones were used in Britain. The introduction of the railways changed all this. Accurate timetables were needed to make sure that people did not miss their trains. In 1880, all clocks were changed to Greenwich Mean Time (see opposite).

An express train in the 1890s

The GMT clock at Greenwich is used to measure standard time

14

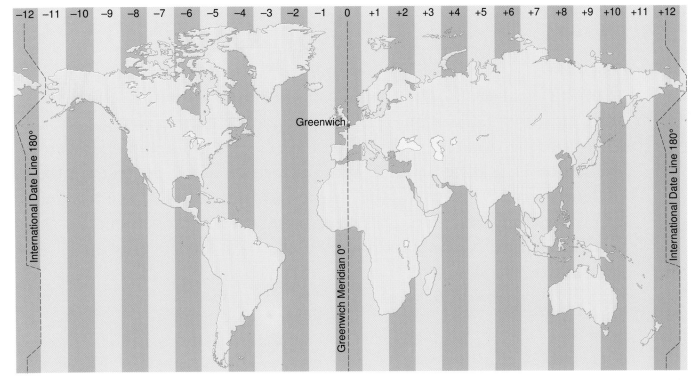

The time zones of the world

GREENWICH MEAN TIME

The Greenwich Meridian is an imaginary line that runs from north to south through Greenwich in London. It is the starting point for all the world's time zones. The Meridian stands at 0° longitude. Distances and times are measured by how many degrees of longitude they are to the west or east of Greenwich. The system of time based on the Greenwich Meridian is called Greenwich Mean Time (GMT) or Universal Time (UT). It is the standard time used throughout the world.

The Greenwich Meridian

INTERNATIONAL DATE LINE

The International Date Line is an imaginary line running from north to south through the Pacific Ocean, along the line of 180° longitude. As you cross the line, the date changes and you lose or gain a whole day. The western side of the line is one day ahead of the eastern side.

IN FACT...

Travelling through time can be an uncomfortable business. Your body has its own built-in clock which tells you when to go to sleep and when to wake up. If you fly a long way west or east you may suffer from jet lag, as your body clock becomes confused about what the time really is.

THE FIRST CALENDARS

Thousands of years ago, people began to organise and plan their time by using a calendar. The earliest calendars were devised by astronomer-priests, in order to plot special religious events and to make sure that sacred rituals were performed at the correct times. Calendars were also used to plan the farming year and the payment of taxes. Most early calendars were based on the movements of the Earth, Sun and Moon which were used to divide the year into months and days.

IN FACT...

Stonehenge is a circle of huge standing stones in southern England, built around 3,500 years ago. Scientists think that Stonehenge might once have been used as a giant calendar, to plot the position of the Sun and the stars, and to calculate the length of the year.

EGYPTIAN DATES

One of the earliest calendars was devised by the Ancient Egyptians some 5,000 years ago. This was the first calendar to divide the year into 365 days. The Egyptians used their calendar to calculate the date of the annual flooding of the River Nile, the vital event in their farming year (see page 8). From the movements of the Moon and stars, the astronomer-priests worked out that the river flooded on average every 365 days, roughly the same length of time as a solar year (see page 11). The Egyptian year was divided into 12 months of 30 days each, with five extra days at the end of the year.

COUNTING THE YEARS

The Ancient Egyptians counted their years from the date when a new pharaoh (king) came to the throne. As each pharaoh was crowned, the calendar began again at year 1.

THE MANDATE OF HEAVEN

In Ancient China, the calendar was used to make sure that the empire ran smoothly. The Chinese believed that the gods would look after their empire so long as the emperor worshipped the gods at the correct times. This contract between the gods and the emperor was called the Mandate of Heaven. In order to fulfill the Mandate of Heaven, the emperor had to perform his daily rituals and offerings to the gods at exactly the right times. Otherwise the empire would collapse.

MAYAN TIMEKEEPING

The Maya of Central America had two very accurate calendars. Their everyday calendar was based on the solar year, with 18 months of 20 days each and five odd days. They also had a sacred 260-day calendar for showing special religious days and festivals. The Maya thought of the days, months and years as burdens carried on the backs of the gods who marched in relays along a road with no beginning and no end. For the Maya, this was how time passed.

The Mayan sign for the date 11 February AD 256. The animals represent blocks of time; the gods represent numbers.

A modern Chinese calendar, using standard days, weeks and months

AZTEC DAYS

The Aztecs adopted the Mayan calendar. They gave each day a special value, ranging from good days to evil days. The five extra days needed to complete the year were particularly unlucky. They were not given names or numbers but were known as 'left over and profitless days'.

A modern copy of an Aztec calendar

CHANGING THE CALENDAR

Most ancient calendars had to add on extra days or even an extra month every so often to bring them into line with the true solar year. The Babylonians added three extra months every eight years to keep their calendar in step with the Sun and the Moon. The calendar we use today is called the Gregorian calendar. It was devised in 1582 and was adapted from the Julian calendar. However, the change from the Julian to the Gregorian calendar involved several large adjustments.

An ancient Julian calendar from Roman times, with the months, and the days and dates of the week marked with pegs

THE JULIAN CALENDAR

The Julian calendar was invented by the Roman ruler, Julius Caesar. Originally, the Roman calendar had a 120-day year, divided into four months. But by the time Julius Caesar came to power, the Roman calendar had fallen so far out of step that it no longer matched the seasons. To bring it in line, Caesar ordered that the year 46 BC should last for 445 days. February gained an extra 23 days, and 67 days were added between November and December. Not surprisingly, this year became known as the 'Year of Confusion'!

GAINING TIME

The Julian calendar calculated the length of the year as 365.25 days. To avoid having a quarter of a day left over at the end of each year, most years had 365 days, with an extra day inserted every four years at the end of February. Unfortunately, the Julian year was still 11 minutes and 14 seconds too long. This doesn't sound very much, but it meant that the calendar gained one day every 128 years. Over the centuries, this gain began to become quite noticeable. The solution came in the form of the Gregorian calendar.

Part of a 15th-century German calendar

BREAKTHROUGH

The Gregorian calendar was named after Pope Gregory XIII, who introduced it. In 1582, Pope Gregory decreed that ten days should be lost to put right the gains of the Julian calendar. So in most Catholic countries the day after 4 October 1582 became 15 October 1582. Britain did not adopt the Gregorian calendar until 1752 and in Greece and Russia it was not officially recognised until the early 1900s. The modern Gregorian calendar measures time extremely accurately, losing just one day every 44,000 years.

Pope Gregory XIII

SIGNPOST

One of the features of the Julian calendar that still survives today is the extra day, 29 February, added every four years. The year when this occurs is called a leap year. Leap years are always years which divide by four, such as 1992 and 1996. The Gregorian reform added a new rule – no century year is a leap year unless divisible by 400. So in 1900 there was no leap year, but the year 2000 will be a leap year.

A calendar for the year 1884 – a leap year!

MORE CALENDAR CHAOS

By the time that the Gregorian calendar was adopted in Britain in 1752, it was necessary to lose 11 days. The 11 lost days made people furious and there was rioting in the streets. People thought the government was trying to cheat them out of 11 days' wages.

FAMOUS NAMES

In the 19th century, the French philosopher, Auguste Comte, came up with another new idea for the calendar. He suggested having 13 months of 28 days each, with an extra day at the end. He also renamed each day, week and month after a famous historical figure, including Homer, St Paul, Shakespeare and Aristotle. The idea never caught on!

RELIGIOUS CALENDARS

Each of the world's major religions has its own calendar for recording religious events, and setting dates for festivals, rituals and pilgrimages. People in ancient times were extremely careful about performing ceremonies and offerings to the gods at the correct times. Otherwise these rituals might not be effective and the gods might be angry.

Brahma, the Hindu god of creation

HINDU CALENDAR

In India, the ancient Hindu calendar is used in religious life and the Gregorian calendar in everyday life. Hindus see the world as a series of cycles of time. One cycle equals 12,000 divine years. One divine year is 360 solar years, so this makes a total of 4,320,000 years. A thousand of these cycles makes one *kalpa*. This is equivalent to a single day in the life of the god Brahma, the creator of the universe.

JEWISH CALENDAR

The Jewish calendar dates from 3761 BC, the supposed date of the creation of the world. This calendar is based on the phases of the Moon. The Jewish religious day begins and ends at sunset. Saturday is the Shabbat, or holy day.

IN FACT...

In the ancient Jewish calendar, 50 was a holy number. Every 50 years, people were released from their debts and slaves were given their freedom.

The Mount of Olives in Jerusalem, where ancient Jewish priests lit a fire to mark the appearance of the full Moon.

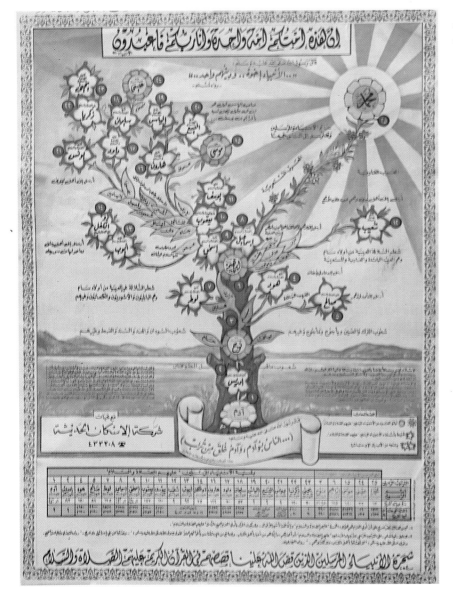

A Muslim calendar, decorated with a tree showing the descendants of the prophet Muhammad

Easter is one of the most important times in the Christian year when Christians remember Christ's death on the cross and his resurrection from the dead. But early Christians could not agree on the date for Easter. In AD 325, it was decided that Easter should fall on the first Sunday after the first full Moon on or after the spring equinox (around 20 March). This means that Easter can vary by over a month, from 22 March to 25 April.

An Easter procession in Seville, Spain

THE YEAR IN ISLAM

The Muslim calendar begins on 16 July AD 622, the date on which the prophet Muhammad fled from the city of Mecca to Medina to escape from his enemies. This journey is known as the Hijrah and the calendar as the Hijri. Each month begins with the new Moon, and the Muslim year is 11 days shorter than the Gregorian year. The year 1996 in the Gregorian calendar corresponds to year 1416 in the Hijri. The most important month in the Muslim calendar is Ramadan, the holy month of fasting. During this month people are not supposed to eat or drink between sunrise and sunset.

EARLY TIMEKEEPERS

The very first timekeepers were natural clocks, such as the Sun, Moon and stars. Gradually, people began to use other, man-made devices for telling the time. These included sundials, shadow clocks, water clocks and candles.

An Egyptian shadow clock from about 1000 BC

Part of the giant sundial in the royal observatory, Jaipur, India

SHADOW CLOCKS

The Ancient Egyptians invented shadow clocks, the earliest clocks known, some 4,000 years ago. The shadow clock was T-shaped and the time was shown by the shadow of the crossbar falling across a marked-out time scale. The Egyptian pharaoh, Tuthmosis III, may have carried a portable shadow clock into battle with him.

SUNDIALS

Sundials were invented in Egypt in about 800 BC. As the Sun shines on an upright or tilted stick, called a gnomon, a shadow is cast on a dial marked in hours. Sundials were also popular in Greece and Rome and were used in Europe well into the 18th century. You can sometimes see large sundials on the walls of churches and old houses. Small, portable sundials were also made for travellers.

WATER CLOCKS

The problem with sundials and shadow clocks was that at night or in cloudy weather they were no good at all. So water clocks were often used instead. In a water clock, the passing of time is indicated by the changing level of water. In Ancient Greece, water clocks were used to limit the length of lawyers' speeches in the law courts!

A Chinese incense clock. The incense burns at a steady rate around the maze-like tray.

SMELLING TIME

Incense clocks were used in China from the 6th century AD right up to the 17th century. Incense burns at a steady rate so is well suited for measuring the hours. In some clocks, different types of incense were used for the different hours so that people could actually smell time passing!

CANDLE CLOCKS

Candle clocks were first used about 1,000 years ago. A candle was marked down the side in hours of equal length. As the candle burned down, you could see how many hours had passed. It is said that candle clocks were invented by Alfred the Great of England.

A candle clock

SANDGLASSES

Hourglasses or sandglasses were widely used in medieval Europe, often on board ships and to time church sermons. The 'sand' was actually powdered eggshell. Real sand was too coarse. The sand trickled through a small hole between two glass bulbs to measure a fixed amount of time.

❑N FACT...

The Romans may have invented the world's first talking clock. This was a man in the forum (market place) of a town who was employed to shout out the time. Wealthy Romans also used slaves to read out the time from their private water clocks.

A set of four sandglasses, ranging from a quarter of an hour (left) to one full hour (right)

SIGNPOST

Water clocks were the first alarm clocks. They were used in medieval monasteries to set off an alarm to wake up the monks for prayers.

THE FIRST MECHANICAL CLOCKS

As towns expanded and trade became more organised, people needed more accurate ways of telling the time. The first mechanical clocks were built in Europe in the late 13th century. Soon public clocks had appeared in many town and market squares. Personal clocks and watches followed later.

LIKE CLOCKWORK
Early mechanical clocks were driven by a device called a verge escapement. Inside the clock, a set of wheels was turned by a falling weight on a cord. Two metal rods controlled the speed at which the wheels turned and moved the hands around the clock face.

SWINGING TIMES
The first pendulum clock was made in 1657 by the Dutch scientist, Christiaan Huygens. It was the most accurate mechanical clock so far and the first to measure seconds. Inside this type of clock, a pendulum swings back and forth at a steady, even beat. This regular movement turns the wheels which control the hands of the clock.

An early pendulum clock, designed by Huygens

A clockmaker at work

CLOCKS FOR CARRYING

The first pocket watch was invented in Germany in 1504. The watch was small and light enough to fit in a waistcoat pocket. Wristwatches were not made until 1790. At first, pocket watches were expensive luxuries. But in 1868, a firm of Swiss watchmakers designed a cheaper pocket watch that ordinary people could afford.

One of the earliest pocket watches, shown with its silver case

CLOCKMAKING CENTRES

Early mechanical clocks were handmade from iron by locksmiths and blacksmiths. But as the demand for clocks increased, guilds of specialist clockmakers grew up. The most famous early centres of clockmaking were Italy and Germany but they were soon overshadowed by the clockmakers of Switzerland, where some of the finest clocks are still made.

PRECISION TIMING

Today, time can be measured extremely precisely. The most accurate modern timekeeper is an atomic clock developed in the early 1990s. It loses or gains just one second every 1.6 million years! Clocks and watches are now cheap to buy and available in all shapes and sizes.

Alexander Bain

BREAKTHROUGH

Quartz clocks were first made in 1929. They contain tiny crystals of quartz which vibrate and act like pendulums when they are charged with electricity. The vibrations control the speed of an electric motor which turns the clock hands. Sometimes the time is displayed as numbers on a screen, called a digital face.

This scientific quartz clock is used to measure time to an accuracy of one-thousandth of a second per day.

CLOCKS GO ELECTRIC

The first electric clock was developed in 1840, by a Scottish clockmaker, Alexander Bain. It was battery powered. Mains-powered electric clocks were first produced in the USA in the early 1900s.

ATOMIC ACCURACY

The most accurate timekeepers ever made are atomic clocks. The first atomic clocks were made in 1948. These clocks are driven by vibrating atoms of ammonia gas or the metal, caesium. They are used by scientists to measure time extremely precisely.

COUNTDOWN

The Doomsday clock is a nuclear clock designed in 1947 to count down to midnight and the nuclear holocaust which it was thought could end the world. Today, the clock stands at 17 minutes to midnight. But it can run backwards as well as forwards. At the height of the Cold War between the former USSR and the USA, the hands stood at two minutes to midnight!

IN FACT... An extremely accurate electronic timing device inside a camera is used to give split-second times for sprint races, horse races and other sporting events. The winner may be just one-hundredth of a second faster than the runner-up.

A split second makes the difference between winning and losing a race.

KEEPING WATCH

Wristwatches are like miniature clocks. The first quartz watches were made in 1967 and the first digital watches four years later. The great thing about these watches is that they are battery-powered and do not need winding every day. Today you can buy quartz watches which not only tell the time and date, but have stopwatches and calculators in them as well. Solar-powered watches are also available.

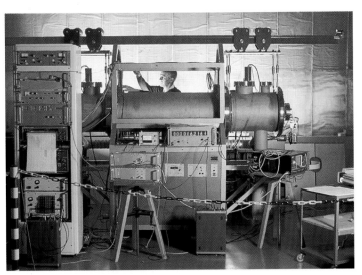

Wristwatches

SECONDS AWAY

As a result of the amazing accuracy of atomic clocks, the whole way of telling time has been rethought. Before the development of atomic clocks, timekeeping was based on the Earth's rotation which changes slightly all the time. This meant that all clocks were slightly inaccurate. In 1967, a new definition of time was agreed. Whereas a second had been defined as 1/86,400th of a day, it was now redefined as the time taken for an atom of caesium to vibrate 9,192,631,770 times.

A caesium atomic clock – the most accurate clock in the world

TIME TAPE

GLOSSARY

AD Stands for *Anno Domini* which means 'in the year of our Lord'. AD is used to indicate years after the birth of Christ.

Astrologer A person who studies the stars and planets in order to predict the future.

Astronomer A scientist who studies space and the heavenly bodies (planets, stars, moons, comets, asteroids and so on).

Axis An imaginary line that runs through the centre of a planet. The planet rotates, or spins, around its axis.

BC Stands for 'Before Christ'. BC is used to indicate years before the birth of Christ.

Caesium A soft metal, with a golden sheen.

Digital A digital clock or watch has a screen which shows the time in numbers, rather than hands which move around a clock face.

Eclipse When the Sun or Moon is blocked out by another heavenly body passing in front. In ancient times, eclipses were thought to be very unlucky signs.

Equinox The times at which the Sun crosses the Equator and day and night are equal in length. The spring equinox happens on about 20 March; the autumn equinox on 22 or 23 September.

Gnomon The upright or tilted stick on a sundial which casts a shadow on to the dial.

GMT (Greenwich Mean Time) The time at the Greenwich Meridian, used as the standard for time throughout the world.

Greenwich Meridian An imaginary line which runs through Greenwich in London and marks the line of 0° longitude and the starting point of the world's time zones.

Gregorian calendar The calendar we use today, devised by Pope Gregory XIII in 1582.

Horoscope A chart showing the position of the stars and planets at the time of a person's birth. Astrologers claim to be able tell a person's future from their horoscope.

Jet lag The feeling of disorientation caused by your internal body clock becoming confused as you travel a long way east or west.

Julian calendar The calendar devised by the Roman ruler, Julius Caesar. It began on 1 January 45 BC.

Leap year Every four years there is a year of 366 instead of the usual 365 days. The extra day is needed to make up for the fact that the Earth takes slightly longer than 365 days to orbit the Sun.

Lunar To do with the Moon.

Pendulum A long rod with a weighted end which swings at an even pace to regulate the ticking of a clock.

Portable Small and easy to carry about.

Quartz A type of mineral (chemical) which forms clusters of crystals inside rocks.

Solar To do with the Sun.

Solar year The time taken for the Earth to orbit the Sun: 365 days, 5 hours, 48 minutes and 45.9747 seconds.

Time zone A division of the Earth with its own fixed time. The world was divided into 24 time zones in 1884.

INDEX